IDEA WISE Garages

Inspiration & Information for the Do-It-Yourselfer

Laura F. Gross

Creative Publishing
international

CHANHASSEN, MINNESOTA
www.creativepub.com

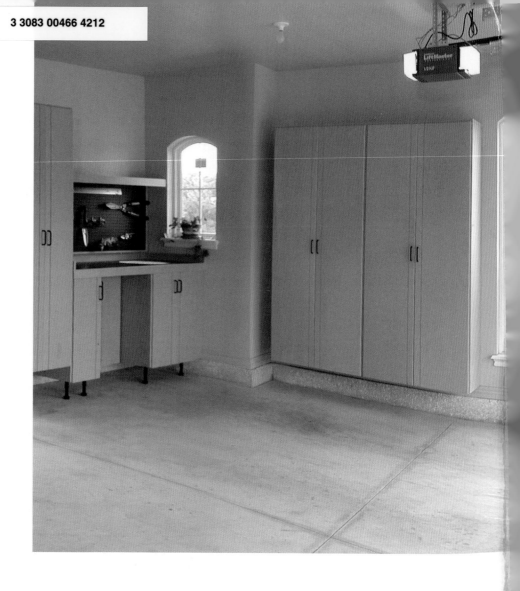

**Creative Publishing
international**

Copyright © 2005
Creative Publishing international, Inc.
18705 Lake Drive East
Chanhassen, Minnesota 55317
1-800-328-3895
www.creativepub.com
All rights reserved

Printed in China

10 9 8 7 6 5 4 3 2 1

President/CEO: Ken Fund
Vice President/Publisher: Linda Ball
Vice President/Retail Sales & Marketing: Kevin Haas

Executive Editor: Bryan Trandem
Creative Director: Tim Himsel
Managing Editor: Michelle Skudlarek
Editorial Director: Jerri Farris

Author: Laura F. Gross
Art Director: Kari Johnston
Mac Designer: Jon Simpson
Project Manager: Tracy Stanley
Photo Acquisitions Editor: Julie Caruso
Cover Photographer
 and Location Scout: Andrea Rugg
Copy Editor: Linnéa Christensen
Technical Illustrator: Rich Stromwall
Production Manager: Laura Hokkanen

IdeaWise: Garages

Library of Congress
Cataloging-in-Publication Data

ISBN 1-58923-182-1

Table of Contents

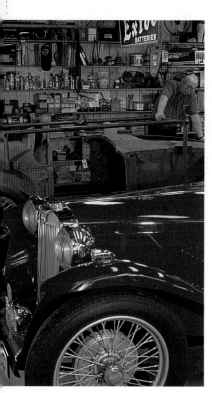

Introduction

The story of the garage is actually a love story.

A few hundred years ago, there were virtually no garages. They weren't missed. We had no cars, and not much in the way of other belongings, to put in a garage should we have built one.

Times have changed. Today, according to the U.S. Bureau of Transportation Statistics, each of the 107 million households in America possesses an average of 1.9 cars, trucks, or sport utility vehicles. All of those vehicles must be housed, and so we have garages.

Boy, do we have garages. A survey sponsored by the National Association of Home Builders brings us this statistic: 83 percent of new homes being built today include garages that hold at least two cars. By 1990, 70 percent of new homes had two-car garages, and only 10 percent were built with single-car garages. By 1992, there were more new homes built with three or more garages than with single garages. By the end of the 1990s, 16 percent of new homes were built with garages big enough for three or more cars.

That's impressive. But we're not done when the garage has been built. Oh, no. According to the NAHB, the market for garage remodeling and organization is $2 billion and growing fast.

Interestingly, at the same time that the money spent on building and outfitting garages has been growing, domestic car sales have been dropping. The explanation? We simply love our garages.

The word "garage" comes from a French word, *garer* which means "to park." Although most of us have garages, far too few of us actually park there every day. In many homes, the garage is filled to the brim with scooters, skateboards, bats and balls, sticks and gloves, lawn mowers, snowblowers, paint cans and brushes, stuff we've just bought and stuff waiting to be thrown away.

That's where this book comes in. *IdeaWise Garages* was written to help you find a place for every thing in your garage and ways to keep every thing in its place. With a bit of planning, a little cleaning and clearing, and possibly some remodeling, you can make your garage into whatever your heart desires: more space to live, play, entertain, store your belongings, and yes, possibly, even park.

In the following pages, we'll guide you through more than a hundred garages, pointing out ideas and details that may not have occurred to you. Along the way, we'll define a few terms, describe ways you can get the most for your remodeling dollars, and suggest specific, doable project ideas.

Mattel Toys

Hewlett-Packard

Before we start looking ahead, let's take a brief look back at the history of garages, starting with the part one particular garage played in the birth of the automobile. In 1896, Ford produced his first "horseless carriage" in a neighbor's garage.

By 1913, Ford had installed the first moving assembly line in the Ford Motor Company. By the time the stock market crashed in 1929, 23 million Americans owned cars. In the 1930s, the first attached one-car garages nestled up to new homes in all parts of the country. By 1940, the attached garage—beloved for its convenient access to the kitchen—finally outnumbered detached garages.

As its popularity grew, the garage continued to inspire greatness. Maybe it's the relative isolation of the garage; perhaps its starkness; perhaps simply its availability. Whatever the reason, the garage has hosted more than a few brilliant, creative oddballs and seen the birth of some of the most important inventions and corporations in history. Among them:

Apple Computers
Delta Airlines
Disney
Hewlett-Packard
Mattel Toys
Polaroid Land Camera
Reader's Digest

Apple Computers

Reader's Digest

Delta Airlines

An amazing catalog of music has been born in garages, too. In fact, garages and bands are inextricably linked in the history of American pop culture. Among others, Buddy Holly, Kurt Cobain, and Soul Asylum got their starts in garages. Barry Gordy, the founder of Motown, worked for Ford before launching his own label, a label with a recording studio in … you guessed it … a garage.

It's not merely the famous and infamous who gather in garages to bang out a beat and play their funky music. Being part of a garage band has practically become a rite of passage for American teens of a certain sensibility. Today, collectors across the country do a brisk trade in obscure garage band recordings, another part of the hold garages have on our collective consciousness.

And so we end up back where we started: today. A time when we have more cars than drivers and still have more garage space than cars to fill it. No big surprise, really. We also have more tools for every task, more hobbies than time to indulge them, and a continuing supply of talented (and semi-talented) folks making music and building dreams in garages across North America. Maybe even yours.

Keep both the history and the future of the garage in mind as you read this book. But most of all, keep in mind what you love about your garage and what you don't. Retain what you love, change what you don't. Fix and fuss and dawdle all you want. You're in good company.

How to Use This Book

The pages of *IdeaWise Garages* are filled with images of interesting, attractive, efficient garages. And although we hope you enjoy looking at them, they're more than pretty pictures: they're inspiration accompanied by descriptions, facts, and details meant to help you plan your garage space wisely.

Some of the garages you see here will suit your sensibilities and circumstances while others may not appeal to you at all. If you're serious about remodeling or building a garage, read every page—there's as much to learn in what you don't like or need as in what you do. Look at the photographs carefully and take note of the details.

IdeaWise Garages contains five chapters: Multi-use, Workshops, Restoration and Display, Conversion to Living Space, and Approaches. In each chapter, you'll find several features, each of which contains a specific type of advice.

DesignWise features hints and tips from professional designers and architects.

DollarWise describes money-saving ideas that can be adapted to your own plans and circumstances.

IdeaWise illustrates a clever do-it-yourself project for each topic.

Another important feature of *IdeaWise Garages* is the Resource Guide on pages 136 to 141. The Resource Guide contains as much information as possible about most of the photographs in the book, including contact information for designers and manufacturers when available.

DesignWise

Don M. Meier
Ciola Meier Construction
Minneapolis, MN

If you plan to do automotive restoration out of the same garage in which you do woodworking, there are several precautions you need to take:

• You can use a woodworking bench for automotive projects as long as you protect your workbench with hardwood or an impermeable material. Grease from a car or motorcycle part left on a workbench will ruin the finish on wood projects.

• Sawdust must be eliminated thoroughly with a dust collection system. Tiny airborne dust particles can wreak havoc on the sensitive fuel and air lines of carburetors and other car parts.

• To protect tools from dust and dirt, store them in drawers as opposed to hanging them in the open.

• Ventilation is critical. Keep the garage door and windows open when working with solvents and other oil-base tools. Check the labels on all solvents and finishes to determine what other safety measures you need to take. Dust masks won't protect you from toxic vapors—use a respirator. Be sure to read all directions carefully if you plan to use a respirator with carbon filters.

DollarWise

Lifts, shelves, and other storage units can significantly improve the functionality of your garage. They also can make parking a challenge. To avoid expensive mistakes, paint brightly colored alignment guides on the garage floor or walls and make sure every driver in the family knows how to use them.

Another good trick is to hang a tennis ball from the ceiling. Position the ball so it's suspended directly in front of the rear view mirror when the car is safely positioned.

IdeaWise

Upper walls and ceilings are ideal spaces for shelves and storage bins, but pulling out a ladder to get to your stuff literally can be a drag.

Instead, mount a library ladder to the front of the shelves. The ladder hangs at the edge of the shelves, well out of the way until you need to use it. Then, roll the ladder into place, and you have safe access to even the highest shelves.

CHAPTER 1

The Multi-use Garage

Very few of us view garages simply as someplace to park anymore. We have bigger plans for this space. At the very least we want a place to store the lawn mower, along with the car. At the most, we want garages with whole rooms—whole suites of rooms—built into the second floor (an idea we'll explore in chapter 4). Reality for most of us falls somewhere in between. We divvy up the space between our cars and some other space-hungry pursuit—a workshop; an office; a place to entertain, rebuild motorcycles, store sporting equipment, start a band, build a computer named for a fruit that will eventually revolutionize the world of technology—whatever.

A garage in which the same space is used for both its traditional purpose—parking the car—and any other purpose is a "multi-use" garage and the subject of this chapter.

Locking cabinets protect possessions and people, especially children. Power tools, poisonous or toxic chemicals, and combustible materials should be stored in locked cabinets.

Rolling bases can be stored at the perimeter then pulled into a convenient working arrangement when a project is underway.

A well-organized, well-planned garage offers space for many activities. This oversized, three-car garage serves as a play space for children, a workshop for adults, and a storage space for hobby and seasonal items.

A regular entry door provides easy access without opening the overhead doors, a welcome convenience when children are running in and out after bikes and sports equipment.

Heavy-duty shelves hold seasonal items such as a snowblower, sleds, and cushions for the lawn furniture.

Between the house and garage, a steel door with an automatic closer helps keep automobile exhaust, dust, and other vapors out of the house.

Take advantage of otherwise-wasted space: Tuck racks above the tracks for an overhead garage door. These shelves hold about 250 pounds each.

*Idea*Wise

Upper walls and ceilings are ideal spaces for shelves and storage bins, but pulling out a ladder to get to your stuff literally can be a drag.

Instead, mount a library ladder to the front of the shelves. The ladder hangs at the edge of the shelves, well out of the way until you need to use it. Then, roll the ladder into place, and you have safe access to even the highest shelves.

A plywood floor and lightweight shelving
converted this garage attic to ideal storage space, reserving
precious floor space in the garage for other purposes. One
caveat—store only items that can be exposed to temperature extremes safely. Garage attics can experience swings of
more than 100° F from summer to winter in some climates.

Multi-use garages cry out for floors that look good and clean up easily. One good option is an epoxy finish on a traditional concrete floor.

There are dozens of epoxy floor coating products on the market. Research your options thoroughly—some need repainting in a year; others can last a decade.

A do-it-yourself epoxy coating kit for a one-car garage floor costs about $60 to $120 and includes a concentrated cleaning solution (the floor has to be extremely clean or the epoxy won't adhere properly), the epoxy coating, decorative color chips, and detailed instructions.

Plan on paying extra if you need to patch cracked cement before you paint or want to add non-skid material to the epoxy coating. (Cement floors can be very slippery when wet if you don't include a non-skid additive.)

THE MULTI-USE GARAGE

If you don't want to deal with applying an epoxy coating and are willing to spend a bit more on your garage floor, consider a floor mat. Several companies now make heavy-duty polyvinyl mats. These mats are meant to drive on, even with studded snow tires. They cover cracks and stains and are impervious to oil, battery acid, anti-freeze, and other damaging substances. Depending on the thickness (between .05 and .09"), these mats cost about $1.40 to $2.40 per square foot.

It's easy to install garage flooring yourself, either in selected areas or wall to wall. Even the thickest mats can be trimmed easily, and although you can use adhesive if you want, it isn't necessary.

Another, somewhat pricier garage floor option is textured rubber, interlocking floor tiles. These tiles are easy to lay out and maintain.

You can easily create racing stripes or checkered patterns with colored tiles.

Texture makes garage floor covering slip resistant.

Heavy-duty floor mats on each side of the door protect floors and give family members a place to change shoes.

Pegboard offers an almost infinite number of places to hang tools and toys.

Organization is the key to using one space for a variety of activities. The space in this garage is loosely divided into activity centers—a household workshop, a car and motorcycle maintenance workshop, and a gardening center. Because the area is also used as a play space for young children, tall cabinets are especially important—they provide space to keep hazardous materials and power tools out of reach.

Sealed concrete repels motor oil, anti-freeze, and other chemicals, a valuable characteristic in a garage used to maintain as well as store cars and other motor vehicles.

Find ingenious ways to store your toys.

A hand-pulled bike hoist like this has a 45-lb. capacity and costs only about $35. Look for a lift with a self-locking cam; a locking cam ensures that if you accidentally let go, the pulley stops automatically to prevent the bike from falling. With a vertical lift of eight and a half feet, you can even store bicycles directly above your parked car if necessary.

A four-point utility hoist like this one can lift or lower anything up to 90 pounds. It's especially handy for lifting and storing items directly off a vehicle roof. Like the bike hoist, it has an 8.5 ft. lift and self-locking cam.

Supports for heavy-duty lifts must be secured to framing studs with plenty of screws or other hardware rated to carry significant loads.

For vehicles up to 1,000 pounds, consider a motorized lift. The lift bed is 4 × 8' and lifts up to six feet off the floor. You won't need to reinforce the wall because the force is distributed 80 percent to the floor and 20 percent outward from the wall. That gives a maximum of 250 to 300 pounds outward pull on the wall. With a full load, the lift draws 4 amps from a standard 115-volt outlet.

Sturdy railings keep kids and balls where they belong.

A low stucco wall separates the play area from the entertaining area without cutting off the view.

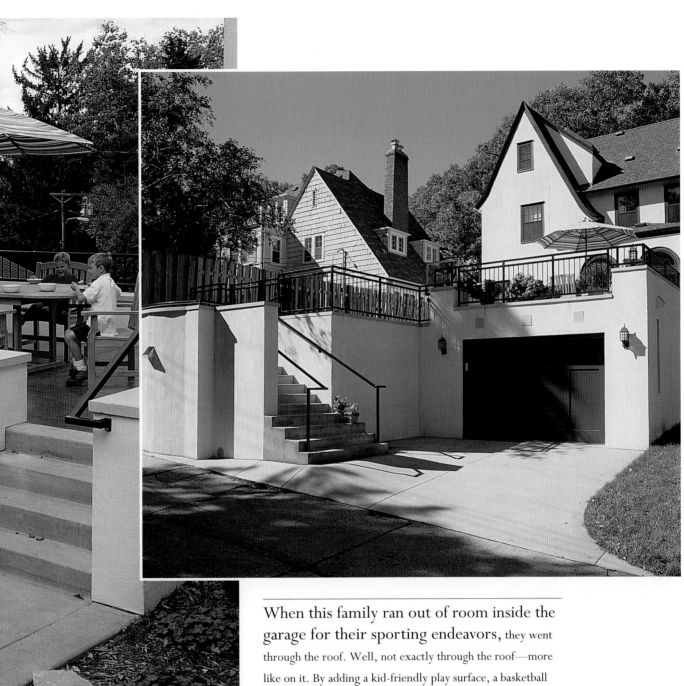

When this family ran out of room inside the garage for their sporting endeavors, they went through the roof. Well, not exactly through the roof—more like on it. By adding a kid-friendly play surface, a basketball hoop, and carefully placed planters and walls, they turned the flat roof of their attached garage into a playground.

Low-maintenance landscaping creates the look of a park without significant groundskeeping.

This garage started life as an ordinary, detached garage facing an alley in a lovely neighborhood with mature trees. The home-owner added translucent panels on one side to bring light into the space.

Next, the framing was extended out and up to add a much-improved version of a play fort. Now, the cars occupy the main garage space, yard and garden tools find homes in the bumped-out section, and children exercise their bodies and imaginations in the fort.

Gardening &
Lawn Care

The $22 billion U.S. lawn and garden market proves we are a proud and picky nation when it comes to the greenery immediately surrounding our homes. It's almost impossible to own a home without a slow creep of lawn/garden care equipment and products gathering valuable space over time. Before investing further space (and dollars) in a standalone shed, assess your garage walls. Can you turn this space into vertical storage?

In sight and within reach:
The two key words in lawn and garden storage are visibility and accessibility. Grid storage systems are particularly appropriate for lawn and garden tools.

A dedicated storage cabinet helps keep potting tools and small planters organized and off the floor. Look for heavy-duty cabinetry that can stand some wear and tear.

*Design*Wise

Karen Law,
K. Law Consulting
Design/Professional Organization
Minneapolis, MN 55410

• Clear it all out and sort everything into piles of like items.

• Divide the garage into zones that fit your work and lifestyle. (Don't set aside a wood shop area if you don't like working with wood, for example.)

• If it's broken, send it to the repair shop or throw it out!

• Have a garage sale and make some money on the items no longer needed.

• Organize the remaining items. Hang it, hook it, get it off the floor.

• Donate items you no longer use. Many charities will pick up donated items. Some communities have Internet bulletin boards where people trade unwanted items.

• Involve the whole family. In most families, every member is part of the problem, and everyone needs to be part of the solution.

• Containerize. Use bins, stackable totes, and containers as much as possible.

• Label every container with a list of its contents.

• Put all poisons and hazardous items in locking cabinets and keep them locked.

• Add plenty of light. You can't use what you can't find.

Floor-to-ceiling, wall-mounted slatted panels are gaining popularity for garage storage. Made of heavy PVC, the panels interlock with a tongue-and-groove design. The panels come in sections that are 15" high and either 4 or 8' wide. Once mounted, they're incredibly strong and can be fitted with a number of accessories, including cabinets, shelves, and specialized bins.

A place for everything, and everything in its place.

Pull-out shelves make the contents of this cabinet very easy to access. If you're not lucky enough to have a storage unit like this, add pull-out shelves to a standard shelf unit. Many models are available from stores that specialize in organization.

Stock or ready-to-assemble cabinets work beautifully in a gardener's work area.

Washable, durable, and inexpensive, a laminate countertop is ideal for a potting table.

Adjustable shelves allow the user to tailor the space to the contents.

In a temperate climate or heated garage, grow lights give a gardener a jump start on the season.

If you're a serious gardener, consider custom cabinetry to store soil, repot and sprout seedlings. Life's short. Indulge your pastime efficiently.

THE MULTI-USE GARAGE

Even the garage's gutters get into the act, directing rainwater into collection barrels. Hoses connected to the barrels let the homeowners use the runoff to water their garden.

Naturally, wheelbarrows can withstand exposure to the weather, so storing them against the side of the garage works fine.

A potting bench nestles under the eaves, providing a pleasant, shady spot to work.

Abutting the garden, this garage is positioned to double as a garden shed. Rather than using precious indoor space, the homeowners put the outside walls to work. The large overhang shelters garden tools and necessities as well as the family's firewood.

Entertaining

Once you get the garage organized and de-cluttered, back the cars out—it's time to party. The party's here, no matter what the weather. There's plenty of room, even in a standard two-car garage, if entertaining essentials are arranged along the walls to maximize the remaining floor space.

Who would guess that this beautiful party space is in the garage? From the cabinetry to the wall coverings, every detail contributes to a beautiful entertaining space.

Washable mats protect the floor beneath the vehicles. Before parties, the mats can be pulled into the driveway and hosed down, if necessary.

A wall-mounted vacuum stands ready for easy clean-up before and after parties.

Built-in cabinets house storage

for entertaining necessities such as a bar,
mini-fridge, and electronics.

Sliding doors disappear into the cabinet during parties, then move into position to protect the electronics and glassware after the party.

A sound system provides music to work or play by.

Entertain in style and comfort.

After completing a spacious deck in the backyard, these homeowners installed a window and a door leading to the deck from their attached garage. The immediate access makes parties more fun for hosts and guests alike.

CHAPTER 2

Garage Workshops

When it comes to garage workshops, the only constant is their location. Beyond that, these spaces are highly personal. The majority of workshops are the domain, primarily, of one person. Gratefully, the workshop is neither a "family" space nor an area of the home that must be kept presentable for visitors or any other reason.

Because it's a creative space, the only thing it must do is suit the creator's needs. That's you. So what do you need? Some people need immaculate workspace; for others the key to the creative process is not having to worry about picking up after themselves immediately. Some take great joy in a system that keeps every tool out of sight until needed; others prefer to hang tools in the open to grab quickly with little forethought.

Individual expression is particularly important in the workshop. If you're the mad scientist/talented tinkering type, create a visually rich environment—even if it makes no sense to anyone else. If you're a precision-loving, Type A, clean freak, you probably need a very different kind of workshop. This chapter won't attempt to persuade you there is one right or best kind of workshop; it simply lays out options to help you maximize efficiency, comfort, and safety, *in accordance with your personal style!*

Most garage workshops follow an organic growth pattern, gathering more tools and increasingly sophisticated machines over time. Most have a combination of old tools—even inherited tools—and thoroughly new fangled gizmos. Honor this growth process; treasure the tools and equipment passed down to you. Your workshop is as much a shrine to your personal history as it is a place to make stuff.

No longer used for parking, this detached garage workshop belongs to an artist who restores antique furniture for a living. Because his work with furniture requires metal and wood-working, he has set up separate workspaces for each.

In most areas, heating is essential for a year-round workshop. Heating is generally measured in British thermal units. (BTUs). To calculate the BTU needs of your workshop, there are a few considerations to take into account including the amount of insulation, the exposure to shade and direct sunlight, and the number and location of windows.

Fluorescent lights are the most inexpensive and energy efficient lighting option for home workshops. They last ten times longer than incandescent lighting and use one-quarter to one-third of the energy.

Opposite the workshop

area in the same garage, the artist
has set up a small relaxation space
for taking breaks.

*Track lighting allows you
to direct "spot light" type
lighting wherever you
want to emphasize an
area of the wall or simply
create visual texture.*

*A couple of floor rugs
over the cement floor go a
long way toward adding
visual warmth to this
area of the garage.*

*An awning window provides
light and ventilation for
the relaxation space.*

Keeping tools in plain sight works better than storing them in drawers for some people, but you really need a private—or at least, secure—garage space to do this since you're not going to be able to lock them up after each use. Tools hung in size order, like these combination wrenches, are easy to keep track of and can be accessed immediately when needed.

Here we see multi-purpose metal mesh material put to use as a homemade, highly practical non-flammable pegboard. The artist attached strips of heavy conduit to the studs through the wallboard at 2-ft. intervals. He then screwed the mesh to the conduit. He uses regular pegboard hooks to hang his tools onto the mesh.

The artist uses this workbench for furniture restoration and other metal work. For projects that involve cutting and welding with a gas torch, a metal workbench is essential.

The exterior of the artist's garage workshop

brings up the question: What do you do with a driveway once your garage is no longer used for parking? If you've replaced the garage door with a wall, windows, or another type of door, you'll need to do something with the driveway. In this case, the property owner replaced the driveway with a trench for backing in and loading up pickups. If this were an attached garage facing forward, the driveway could be replaced by landscaping.

How Big?

Do you have enough space in your garage for a workshop?

Space allocation is a widely variable aspect of the garage workshop. A single garage stall measures roughly 200 square feet. That's plenty of space to set up a workshop. In fact, you can make a perfectly functional workshop with just 150 square feet of floor space. This is enough room for a workbench, a few full-sized tools, and space left over for lumber storage. The space doesn't have to be rectilinear. You can organize a linear work area against one wall of the garage if that's the space available.

With just 300 square feet, you can eke out a really great mid-sized home shop with quite a few large machines.

Anything over 400 square feet is simply not necessary for any but the most serious workshop denizen.

Built into a single-stall attached garage, this workshop is just 220 square feet. No cars allowed here. The homeowner considers this his private space, over which he reigns completely. Anything he leaves out, stays out until he returns.

By lining cabinets along one wall you gain floor-to-ceiling storage without losing floorspace.

Organization & Storage

The need for workshop organization varies greatly. This is where individual proclivities have the greatest impact. Here are a few basic guidelines.

Ideally, you want to use about one-third of your workshop space for storage. Cabinets are the most immediate, easiest solution for storage. It's getting easier to find excellent, durable, reasonably priced cabinetry for garage workshops.

Constructed from high and medium density fiberboard, this system of matching wall-mounted cabinetry and floor units is a great option if an uncluttered, uniform workspace is important to you.

Adjustable-height feet compensate for an uneven floor to keep storage cabinets level.

This wheel-mounted mobile unit fits under the workbench. The top drawer is 2", the middle drawers are 4" and the bottom drawer is 8". All drawers ride on full-extension ball bearing slides for smooth operation.

To compensate for uneven floors, the workbench has threaded bolt leveler pads to allow height adjustments of up to an inch.

The tall gear box locker has a partition down the middle, allowing four half-width shelves to be adjusted at varied heights. It holds up to 300 pounds total.

These wall cabinets have four shelves inside. They can hold a total of 200 pounds per cabinet.

The shelf inside this short gear box extends 20 inches beyond the cabinet doors for easy loading and unloading.

Garage refrigerators are built to keep food in the refrigerator chilled, but not frozen, even if your garage temperature drops to 0 degrees Fahrenheit. The freezer cabinet keep items frozen even if the garage temperature climbs to 110 degrees Fahrenheit.

This garbage compactor rolls right up to the mess for easy cleanup.

Workbenches

Workbenches come in a variety of sizes and styles, but basically fit into one of three categories: Traditional benches, utility benches, and portable benches. Traditional benches have extra thick surfaces and sturdy wooden legs that keep the bench stationary and absorb vibration. The top surface is usually hard maple, beech, or other hardwood laminate. Traditional benches are freestanding units, generally about 2 feet wide and 4 to 6 feet long. They also generally come with at least one end vise and bench dogs for holding work pieces securely. Expect to pay about $500 for a good workbench.

If you must use extension cords, use heavy grade cords in the shortest length possible for maximum electrical efficiency.

Keep the bench width to 3 feet or less, and the length not more than about 8 feet.

Slatboard makes a convenient place to hang frequently used tools.

For average-sized people 30" to 40" is a good working height. Be mindful of back strain.

Even small garages have space for a compact workbench. A few square feet at the front of the garage is all that's truly necessary if it's well planned and organized.

*Design*Wise

Dan M. Meier
Ciola Meier Construction
Minneapolis, MN

Garage cabinetry can easily run in the thousands of dollars if you buy it new. Equally functional at a fraction of the cost are recycled kitchen cabinets. Take the old cabinets from a neighbor who's remodeling the kitchen, or look for old cabinets at a re-use center.

Reinforce the back of upper cabinets before screwing them into the studs. Use cement anchors if you're hanging the cabinets on a cement wall.

If you plan to do a significant amount of woodworking, a decent central dust collection system is important. Some exotic hardwoods—such as rosewood and ebony—produce more harmful types of sawdust. You can find portable dust collectors on wheels in all sizes that hook into the ports on most stationary machines.

You can get a pretty decent medium-size dust collector for about $300.

Industrial rubber mats set up in front of the workstation are a less expensive and easier alternative to wall-to-wall flooring or an epoxy finish. These mats come in various sizes, but are most commonly about 2 × 4'. When they get dirty, just haul them into the driveway, hose them down, and bring them back into the garage.

Planers and jointers need to be mobile unless the workshop is very large. Mounted on mobile bases, they can be rolled out to the driveway for large projects.

Unless you live in a desert climate, rust is a serious threat to power tools. There are numerous protectants on the market to deal with this problem. One of the cheapest and most effective solutions is paste wax. Try rubbing some onto your jointer and planer to keep them lubricated and to prevent rust.

Tool Storage

Effective tool storage requires careful management: Dedicate boxes and drawers for small loose tools, drill bits, small hand tools, nuts and bolts, nails, switches, and any other small bits and pieces you accumulate. Unless you have an extraordinary visual memory, label the drawers. It will save you from having to open each and every drawer or box to figure out where you put something. If you can, mount tool cabinets on casters; they'll be easy to move around the garage.

Keep clamps off the floor. You can use cement anchors to attach 2 × 4s to the wall for clamp storage.

For a modest sized tool chest, you could spend anywhere from $50 to $500, depending on the brand. In most cases you get what you pay for. If you get the cheapest box you can find, it will likely rust or break down within a relatively short time. Spending too much may buy you features you never use. Figure out the size and features you really need, then judge the product by the quality of construction details.

Look for a design with a safety feature that prevents drawers from opening if the unit is accidentally tilted or tipped.

Line drawers to keep tools from slipping around and to prevent rust. You can find inexpensive 1/16" polyethylene drawer liners that come in 48 × 25" sheets.

Look for a flip top with a lock on it.

Full-width drawer pulls are a convenient feature for tool drawers.

Graduated drawer depth helps keep small items from getting buried.

Make sure your tool drawers open with ball bearing slides.

The inside of the box as well as the outside should be coated with a baked enamel finish or another corrosion-resistant finish.

These panels come in two sizes: 4' × 15" or 8' × 15". They stack one above the other, with the seam completely hidden under a slot. The cost is approximately $170 per 30 square feet of paneling. You can cut the panels with a regular wood saw, so they're easy to customize. There is a large assortment of different hooks and accessories that you can buy separately.

You can buy 12" shelf brackets that will hold any standard 12" shelf. A pair of these brackets usually costs less than $10.

The next generation of pegboard, these floor-to-ceiling wall-mounted panels were originally conceived for showroom and commercial displays. Now they're available for residential garages and come with hook accessories for every imaginable hand or power tool you might want to hang up.

A set of tip out bins like this runs just under $50. These are great for keeping workshop hardware or sandpaper organized. Each bin is about 5.5 × 7.5".

This 2-ft. long storage rack for hand tools runs about $11. There are a couple different sized holes, so it works for most screwdrivers, wrenches, and pliers.

Heavy-duty magnetic strips run in two sizes: the 13" strip is about $20; the 24" strip costs about $29.

Workshop Wiring

Workshops require two circuits: One for lighting, the other for electrical outlets. Consider installing a third dedicated circuit if you're running an air conditioner or a large electric heater.

Consider installing a smaller subpanel of additional circuit breakers—this option allows you to switch circuits on and off without having to access the main panel. One 15-amp circuit can power the lights in your shop. A minimum of two 20-amp circuits installed in a separate subpanel allows you to run two power tools at the same time and reduces the chance of tripping a circuit breaker from a start-up surge. Consider a subpanel surge protector to protect sensitive components. Unless you're confident in your wiring abilities, consult a licensed electrician before starting any electrical work.

Determine Your Power Needs

You want a circuit rated at least 20 to 30 percent greater than what your tools draw at peak loads.

The peak load amperage is on the tool's label.

Let's say your circular saw is rated at 13.5 amps. 25 percent greater than this number is about 16.9 amps. That means a 20-amp circuit is sufficient to power your circular saw.

You may be required to install outlet receptacles that are protected with a ground fault circuit interrupter (GFCI). A GFCI outlet at the beginning of an outlet circuit protects downstream outlets as well.

Check local codes: Outlets in garage workshops can usually be installed four feet from the floor and spaced at 2-ft. intervals along the wall. This is much higher and closer together than is found in typical residential wiring.

An outlet situated four feet from the floor is convenient for mobile-base or bench-mounted power tools.

Mobile Bases

Mobile bases for large home shop machines are the best way to stay efficient in a home workshop. Look for high quality mobile bases that are easy to dolly when you need to move them, but stay perfectly steady when you have the brakes engaged and are ready to run the tools. A heavy-duty steel, universal mobile base that can support up to 600 pounds on 3" industrial casters runs about $70. These bases are adjustable from roughly 19 × 20" to about 29 × 29".

Air Quality

Vapors from stains, varnishes, or other finishing products are not simply unpleasant, they're toxic. To avoid overexposure, you need fresh air. Chronic, long-term exposure to solvents may cause adverse effects to the liver, heart, and reproductive systems. It can also cause permanent brain and nervous system damage. If your workshop has no windows, install them. Access fresh air!

If cold weather rules out the option of keeping the garage door open, open windows and doorways, set up portable fans to create a cross-breeze, and use ceiling fans to circulate air.

Long-term exposure to sawdust is another health risk you want to avoid. At the very minimum a woodworking shop needs to include a shop vac. If your workshop includes a table saw, sanders, planers, or other prolific dust producers, invest in a dedicated dust collector to capture sawdust and wood debris at the source. Disposable respirators and those with replaceable filters are also good ways to keep wood dust out of your lungs.

Heating the Workshop

If you want to establish a workshop located in an attached garage, you may be able to heat the space by extending the heating system from the house into the workshop. Extending heat ducts is not a very difficult project for an advanced do-it-yourselfer, but you should get professional advice if you've never worked with heating/cooling systems before. Direct-vent space heaters are another excellent options.

Vented units must be permanently located next to an outside wall. Be sure to have your vented space heater professionally inspected once a year to minimize risk of carbon monoxide poisoning through blocked or damaged vents.

Lighting

DollarWise

If the task lighting in your garage is less than ideal, add more when and where it's needed. Buy several inexpensive clamp lights, available at any hardware store or home center. These floodlights are attached to scissor clamps that can be clipped onto to a nearby stud, ceiling joist, or almost anything else. With their reflective metal hoods, they provide a lot of light for a little bit of money.

The ideal workshop lighting plan combines ambient light and general overhead lights to illuminate the general workspace with task lights for workbenches and machines. Fluorescent tubes last ten times longer than incandescent light bulbs, cast five times as much light, and offer a more even, diffused light. If your garage is already rigged for bulb fixtures, or if you prefer incandescent lights for their warm tones, use the highest wattage bulbs the fixtures can handle. Figure on one bulb per 16 square feet of floor space.

These 4-ft. fluorescent shop lights can be very inexpensive—as low as $10 each—but the low-end fixtures have low-quality ballasts that make an irritating buzzing sound. They also take longer to warm up in colder temperatures. You may want to consider investing in higher quality 4-ft. lights with industrial ballasts. They are quieter, warm up more quickly, and ultimately last longer than the less expensive lights.

Under-cabinet fluorescent lights are easy to install, inexpensive, energy-efficient, and practical. Place them near the back of the cabinet to reduce shadows.

*Idea*Wise

Ordinary ceiling-mounted incandescent light bulbs provide reasonable amounts of light in the immediate area under the fixture, but the light drops off quickly, creating shadows. Fluorescents provide diffuse, even lighting, but they cannot be adjusted to focus direct light where you need it.

You can illuminate a work area with fluorescent or incandescent light, but the best solution is to use both. Supply general lighting with fluorescents and use incandescents for more direct task light where it's needed.

Be sure to install fixtures with protective covers over the bulbs if the ceiling is low or if you frequently work with large material such as lumber or car parts.

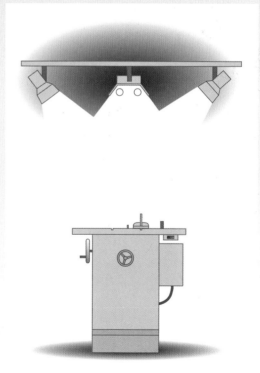

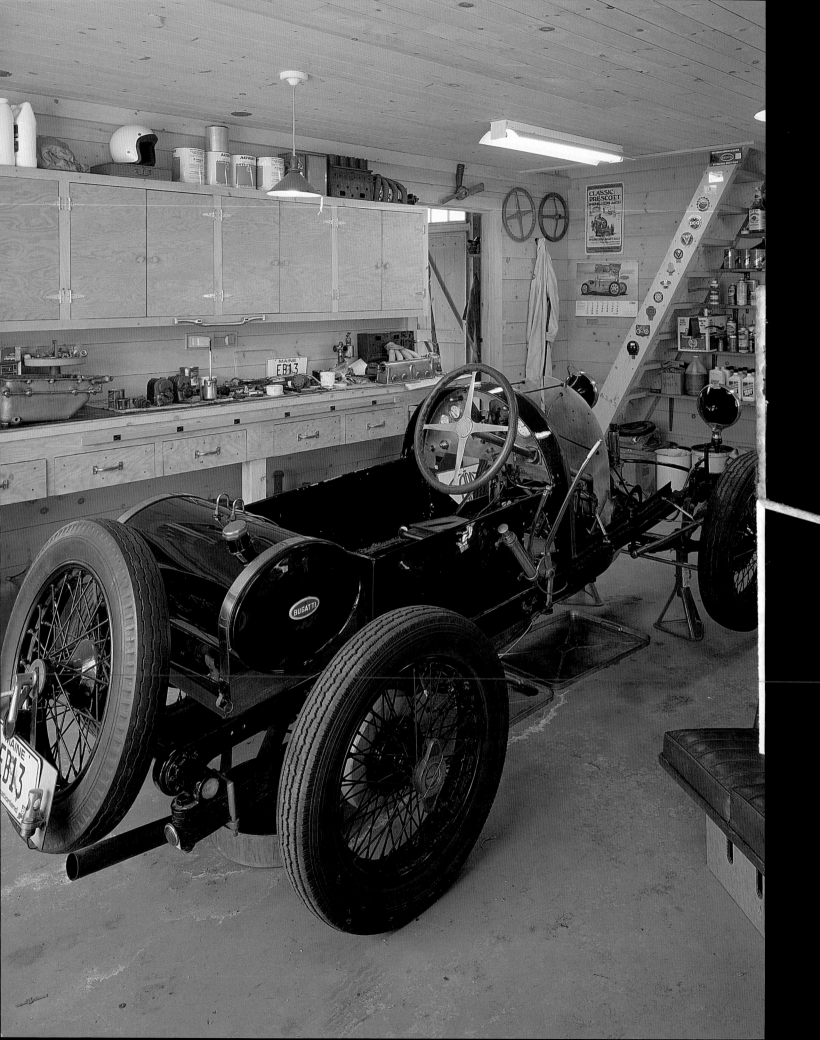

CHAPTER 3

Restoration and Display

For many people, the car sums up the best work of our species: mechanically masterful, sensuously beautiful, powerful, purring, revved up, beloved. And none so beguiles us as the classic car— a breed apart in this heralded herd.

Classics distinguish themselves from their rusting, long forgotten peers through features that capture the imagination of future generations: a stroke of engineering brilliance; breath-taking design. All classic vehicles have some (or many) things that inspire the more talented among us to spend years refurbishing, restoring, refining—bringing the classic back to life. For these, a garage is sanctified space.

The "ultimate garage," as defined by the industry, is basically a showroom for collectors where ultra-violet rays and humidity are as carefully controlled as the restoration process itself. These garages range from 1,000 square feet to 80-car converted airplane hangars and are beyond the means of most car enthusiasts (and this book).

In this chapter we'll look at hidden treasures tucked away behind the doors of ordinary two- and three-car garages in neighborhoods coast-to-coast. Some of these garages host museum-like displays of collectible cars, motorcycles, auto memorabilia posters, and auto-related antiques celebrating the owners' love of a particular type of car, NASCAR, F1, or other racing genre. Others integrate display with the hard work and thorough demands of restoration.

This modest garage exemplifies the hard-working, no-frills restoration shop in which much of the industry's best work is done. Two completed 1947 MGs compete for space with a third that's just gotten underway.

Space Needs

Restoration hobbyists often start off using just one garage stall, quickly spill over into the second stall, and find they're still running short on space. Between the work area, tools, stored parts, and the cars themselves, restoration gobbles space. Unless you have a three-car garage, the family car typically gets demoted to the driveway for the duration of the restoration project (usually a few years). However, if you do have a three-car garage, the newly restored car will get the third parking space before the family car does. Then, of course, there are the vintage gas tanks, ceramic signs, track programs and commemorative tickets, medallions, posters, helmets, driver and crew uniforms, autographs, clocks, and other collectibles. Your family car, frankly, may never see the inside of the garage again once you've succumbed to an auto fetish. Car restoration and collecting is more than a process; it's a culture. Expect—embrace—a bit of sacrifice along the way.

The owner, pictured with his current project, uses his garage to rebuild and restore MGs from the chassis up. Each car takes a couple years. His wife claims she's parked the family car in the driveway for the past 27 years.

This homeowner was able to add a second garage to the right of his larger garage. The family car—at least for now—gets shelter from the elements, as does the coveted classic in the decked out garage beneath the deck.

*Idea*Wise

If your garage floor often gets wet and you're tired of trying to squeegee it dry, a dry well may be the answer. Buy a 5-gallon plastic trash can and use a drill and spade bit to drill holes in it every 8 to 10".

Find the low spot in the garage floor, and draw a circle the size of the trash can on the floor. Use a sledgehammer to break up the concrete, then dig out a hole large enough for the can.

Place the trash can in the hole and fill it with large gravel and other clean rubble, including the concrete you removed from the hole. Mix quick-

drying cement and cover the area, reserving an opening for a standard floor drain cover.

This garage is used not for restoration work, but for display. Along with the vintage car, the owners display automotive, racing, and rock 'n' roll collectibles.

The race deck flooring, pieced together from 10" adhesive-backed resilient tiling, can be installed directly over the cement floor of any garage. This is the same type of scuff-resistant, industrial-use polyvinyl flooring often found in commercial kitchens: It looks great; it's superbly simple to keep clean; it's built tough for years of wear and tear; it protects the cement; it lasts longer than most epoxy coatings; and it doesn't require detailed cleaning or etching prior to installation.

Restoration Tools

Restoration entails refurbishing hundreds of old metal car parts, some as small as bolts and nuts. Many refurbishing tools can be tucked into one corner, as demonstrated here.

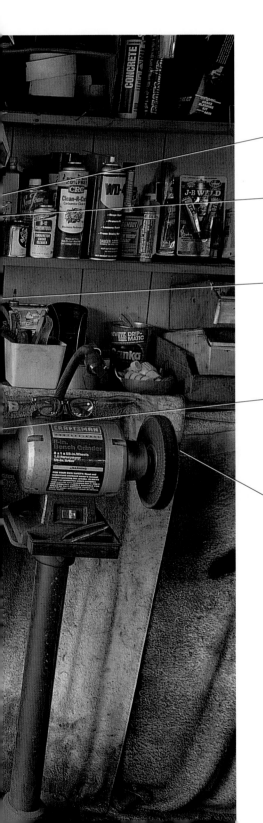

Task lighting makes any job easier. Clamp-on lights offer the most versatile and inexpensive task lighting.

Every garage, especially one used for car restoration, should have at least two fire extinguishers. Look for extinguishers rated for both chemical and electrical fires.

Sandblasting is a common process for stripping paint or rust off old metal parts. Some sandblasters are meant to be used outside, but this type of enclosed sandblaster is housed permanently inside the garage. Sand particles are contained inside the fixture to minimize the mess.

This classic parts washer removes oils and grease from metal pieces. You can scrub metal pieces with wire brushes and rinse them with an articulating stem hose in the basin. The drum is a sump that holds petroleum-based cleaning solution.

There are about 200 different wheels that can be attached to a grinder to perform a range of functions: grinding metal car parts, buffing, wire brushing, and sharpening kitchen knives, to name a few. Though grinders are usually attached to benches, this owner built a stand to give him access to the wheel from all sides of the grinder.

In garages outfitted for restoration, workbenches are generally about 2 feet wide, 4 to 6 feet long, 30 to 40" high, and durable. Beyond that, there's plenty of room for creativity. This workbench was made out of salvaged lumber from a bowling alley. The cabinet it rests on was salvaged from the woman's glove department of a defunct retail store.

RESTORATION AND DISPLAY

This roll-away toolbox stores flush against a wall. The bottom portion is on casters so it can be rolled over to the project. The more organized a person is, the more he or she appreciates the ability to compartmentalize tools according to type and size.

This floor jack needs a hard floor to work correctly. It's not much help on a dirt road or gravel driveway, but great in a garage.

These drawers are lined with a soft, absorbent cork. The cork keeps the tools from sliding around and helps to prevent rust by absorbing excess water that finds its way into the drawer. Some mechanics prefer rubber matting over cork to line their tool drawers.

*Dollar*Wise

There are many terrific shelf, drawer, and display units on the market, some built especially for garage storage. While many of them are wonderfully designed and efficient, they also can be quite expensive.

Before investing in those units, check out local salvage stores, re-use centers, and other secondhand stores. Many communities also have on-line bulletin boards where such items are shared and traded, most often at no charge. You may find unusual solutions for your storage needs.

Overcome challenges with ingenuity.

These homeowners have a passion for vintage motorcycles, mini-bikes, and scooters. Accommodating their hobby requires extremely efficient use of the 20 × 40' garage and the basement beneath it.

The ground-level portion of
this garage houses a collection of vintage
vehicles, the family car, and a home office.

This garage floor is finished in an epoxy
paint to keep the surface superbly clean.

The walls are tiled up to four feet with
12 × 12" ceramic tiles that match the color
of the floor. Everything above the tile line
is painted one color to give the space a
clean and bright uniformity and feeling
of spaciousness.

Setting up a straight-line office along the front wall makes good use of the natural light in this area. In keeping with these homeowners' penchant for a clean, streamlined workspace, the office area is stocked with drawers and cabinets to keep the area clutter free.

The cost of adding a sink to the garage was minimal because it taps directly into the household plumbing stack on the other side of the wall.

This fold-down ladder leads to the storage space above the main floor of the garage. This ladder meets building code because the space it leads to is not considered living space.

A basement beneath the garage provides **much needed space,** but presented several challenges—chief among them the strength required of a garage floor. In this scenario, the floor of the the garage is also the ceiling of this basement shop. This engineering challenge was met by a pre-stressed concrete slab strong enough to bear the weight of the family vehicles despite spanning the shop below.

Exhaust fumes and motor repair are practically inextricable, a challenge for a basement garage. Here, a ceiling fan and nearby windows help ventilate the area.

A portable workbench is more than strong enough to hoist a mini-bike while it's being repaired or cleaned.

Working on dirt bikes can be dirty work. This isn't a problem in most garages, where the dirt can be swept or washed down the driveway. It's more of a challenge in a garage basement, but this large floor drain neatly solves the problem.

Automobilia and Petroliana

Financial professionals are quick to warn that classic cars are a great investment … but only if you really know what you're doing and are careful not to let them take up too much of your portfolio. Compared to traditional investments such as stocks, bonds, or even real estate, vintage vehicles are considered to be a speculative investment. But who cares, really? Getting rich is not the impetus for most vehicle restoration. Rather, it's a fixation, a fascination, a fondness far deeper than the pocket book. This sensibility is what drives the collection of auto-related memorabilia as well, though "automobilia" and its cousin "petroliana" actually are considered a form of investment.

This vintage gas pump belongs to the category of collecting referred to as "petroliana." Within this category are gas pumps, gas pump signs, gas globes, porcelain and tin gas station signs, pump plates, thermometers, oil cans, and other auto-related items from the 1920s through the 1960s. Gas pump replicas cost about $1,000 on average. Restored originals go for as high as $8,000.

The homeowners pictured here installed this '50s era booth—itself a collectible—in the back of their garage to provide a relaxing spot from which to view an impressive display of collectibles.

Vintage racing posters are also part of the collecting culture. (This poster advertises a Mil-waukee Motorcycle racing event from 1962.) Displaying printed material requires a humidity controlled environment.

Surface mounted circuits deliver current to displays throughout the garage. Painted to match the walls, protective conduit blends into the walls.

Paneled walls make attractive **backdrops** for displays of vintage signs and oil cans.

Visitors

Passion—of any type, really—loves company, and none more than a passion for cars.

The collector's culture is a highly social network of like-minded individuals who come together at shows, swap meets, competitions, tours, flea markets, car corrals, and local, regional, national, and even international events of all sorts. However, the most common form of socialization takes place directly in the same garage where these collectors' cars are stored and restored. Expect guests. Plan for them.

If your garage attracts visitors who enjoy a cold one now and then, consider a refrigerated beer dispenser. You'll avoid the clutter of bottles or cans and save money on the cost of beer. Refrigerated dispensers are maintenance free, they last 25 to 30 years, and will keep a keg fresh up to 90 days.

Need help? Open the garage door and pop the hood—you'll get an instant pit crew. Car people are team players. Those with more advanced skills and knowledge are happy to lend a hand.

*Design*Wise

Dan M. Meier
Ciola Meier Construction
Minneapolis, MN

If you plan to do automotive restoration out of the same garage in which you do woodworking, there are several precautions you need to take:

• You can use a woodworking bench for automotive projects as long as you protect your workbench with hardwood or an impermeable material. Grease from a car or motorcycle part left on a workbench will ruin the finish on wood projects.

• Sawdust must be eliminated thoroughly with a dust collection system. Tiny airborne dust particles can wreak havoc on the sensitive fuel and air lines of carburetors and other car parts.

• To protect tools from dust and dirt, store them in drawers as opposed to hanging them in the open.

• Ventilation is critical. Keep the garage door and windows open when working with VOCs and other airborne toxins. Check the labels on all solvents and finishes to determine what other safety measures you need to take. Dust masks won't protect you from toxic vapors—use a respirator. Be sure to read all directions carefully if you plan to use a respirator with carbon filters.

CHAPTER 4

Conversion to Living Space

As homeowners, we love our garages. This is indisputable. But it's also true that we use them for a range of purposes. This makes the garage unique. We can generally agree on the use of a bedroom, bathroom, or kitchen—but the garage? There's no consensus on how best to use it. There are those among us who care little for the historical function of the garage, indeed who view cars as mere vehicles—unworthy of all those unoccupied square feet in the garage. For some, an altogether different passion overtakes automotive concern. These are the homeowners who convert garages into workshops, living space, spas, playrooms, lofts, music studios, party spaces—the list goes on.

Garages are not just for lodging cars anymore, but unfortunately, most are still built as if nothing more is expected to take place in there. Only about 20 percent of garages being built today include livable space; the rest start out cave-like, empty, and uninspired, not intended for human habitation. Herein lies the challenge and the particular creative genius of the American homeowner. We've figured out ways to convert what start out as essentially concrete, windowless bedrooms for cars into functional—sometimes even beautiful—living spaces. This chapter pays tribute to the amazing makeover of what was once the ugly ducking of residential living.

Valuable Spaces

Will converting the garage to livable space increase the value of your home? It depends on whether you're converting the entire garage or just part of it. Conversion may not increase your home's value if there's no parking space left in the garage. Converting the garage into livable space may actually decrease the value of a three- or four-bedroom home. In a smaller home (two bedrooms, let's say), converting the garage is less likely to decrease the resale value of the home. Size is one factor to consider; location is another. If resale value concerns you, ask local Realtors and appraisers how conversions tend to perform in your market.

This comfortable porch added a large amount of living space for a relatively small amount of money. In fact, the overhang was added when the garage was re-sided and re-roofed due to hail damage.

Conversion Costs

Garages are relatively easy and inexpensive to convert to living space. Whether you're working with an attached or detached garage, you've already paid for the excavation, foundation, framing, and closing in the space.

Now let's imagine you begin with a standard 22 × 22' garage that you want to turn into livable space. We're talking about a complete conversion, not shared space—in other words, no more cars in the space. The major factors will be electrical wiring, heating, cooling, windows, doors, and flooring.

If you're an advanced or intermediate do-it-yourselfer, you can probably do everything yourself except perhaps the wiring. (Flooring might also get tricky if the current floor is uneven and/or sloped.) If you do all the labor yourself, you can convert a garage for roughly $7,000, including insulation, windows, subfloor, vinyl floor, baseboard heaters, electric, minimal additional framing and structural lumber, drywall, a new sliding glass door to replace the overhead door, and siding to match the existing siding. If you hire professionals, the same conversion will cost about $16,000.

Attached garages can be easier and less expensive to convert than detached garages. With attached space, you can often extend heating, cooling, plumbing, and wiring from your house.

Home Offices

A recent survey shows that 58 percent of U.S. homeowners would like a home office, though nowhere near that many people work from their homes. For most families, the home office is a place to catch up on bill paying, homework, or work left over from the office.

There are, however, 4 million Americans who work at income-generating jobs exclusively from their homes. For these people, the home office is not a luxury, but a necessity.

Concerns about privacy, noise control, family traffic, and security make converting the garage a tempting option for a home office. Think of what happens when your work is only as far away as the family room: You may check your email after dinner. Then respond. Then notice the invoice you meant to finish. Then print the invoice … and so on. Next thing you know, you've been at your desk an hour, the kids are watching TV instead of doing homework, and you've blown an hour of precious family time. In a garage, the home office is likely to be off the beaten path and less likely to encrouch on your free time.

Half of this garage was converted to office space while the other half remains a traditional garage. For some, a physical separation between home and work is important—even if the separation is only the width of a driveway. If your work includes visits from clients, you'll need a space where you're least likely to be interrupted by others in the household. Business visitors will feel more confident in your professionalism if you keep business as separate as possible from family life.

The home office now residing in half the detached garage is comfortable, practical, and professional.

A conference table doesn't have to be huge but should be at least 4 × 4' to seat four comfortably.

A combination of open cubbies and closed cabinets works best for most home offices.

Built-to-fit (BTF) shelving and cabinets are designed specifically for space that otherwise has no storage. It's the least expensive way to get the maximum (in terms of volume) and most efficient storage into your converted garage office. A combination of open cubbies and closed cabinets work best for most home offices.

Plan plenty of outlets near your computer. Outlets at desktop height help avoid a tangle of hard-to-reach cords behind your desk. As a precaution against blowing a circuit, install two separate circuits. Use surge protectors for your computer and any sensitive electronics.

This converted garage attic is now used for the homeowner's professional sewing and quilting business.

A dormer contributes plenty of light and interesting angles to the room.

Flooring should be matched to the room's purpose. For instance, this smooth flooring makes it easy to find dropped pins and needles.

Flexible track lighting lets you direct light to individual work areas.

Computers are an integral part of many activities, including sewing.

One wall of this converted space is set up as a desk station. Software helps this homeowner generate quilt designs, create and store patterns, and produce elaborate machine embroidery motifs.

Garage Attics

If you want to convert a garage but lot limitations prevent you from expanding outward, go upward instead. Remodeling specialists report seeing a lot more upward expansion in newer homes as a byproduct of larger garage footprints, the expanding demand for storage, and design preferences.

One developing trend in new home construction is to keep garage rooflines even with those of the main residence. This creates essentially a second floor—often called a "bonus room"—above the garage. Bonus rooms are constructed quite specifically to become livable space such as playrooms, family rooms, and home offices.

These expandable garages are not the norm—not yet anyway. At present, the majority of garages still are only a story and a half. The loft space in many garages is suitable for storage, but not always for living space. In a steeply pitched garage attic, there's only enough headroom to stand up straight in the center of the space.

Conversion Costs

For an unfinished garage attic that is 16 × 36' conversion costs between $8,000 to $9,000 if you do the work yourself. This includes insulation, wall and kneewall studs, ceiling joists, pine baseboard trim, a couple of windows, a handrail, 550 square feet of pre-finished, prime grade white oak flooring, electric work, baseboard heaters, drywall (taped and finished), and two pre-hung doors with casing. The cost jumps to around $20,000 if you hire professionals to do the work.

To qualify as "livable" space, building codes in most areas require 7 to 7.5 feet of headroom over at least half the attic space. This measurement means finished floor to finished ceiling. To estimate the headroom in an unfinished attic, measure the distance between the ridge and the joists. If this height is not at least 9 feet, your attic conversion will require either raising the roof or adding dormers to meet code.

Check local building codes for garage roofline restrictions in your area. Your garage may be as tall as it legally can be, in which case raising the roof won't be an option. Dormers, however, may be an option.

Dormers

Dormers dramatically increase the percentage of code-compliant square feet, bring in natural light, and create a ventilation source. If you're thinking about adding a dormer or two, find out first whether your attic floor joists are strong enough to carry the extra weight or if they need to be strengthened. Consult an architect or building contractor to determine joist strength before beginning any work.

The gabled dormers on the garages pictured here integrate effortlessly with the architecture of the residence.

To increase headroom to the maximum extent on their garage attic renovation, these homeowners added shed dormers to each side of the roof. This is a back view; the larger and more decorative of the two dormers faces the street.

Dormers let the sunshine in.

This painter's studio is in the interior of a garage attic. You can see how the steep incline of the roof would severely limit headroom without the addition of the dormer.

A northern window provides steady, muted daylight, ideal for a painter. South-facing windows provide the strongest light.

Window seats are especially welcome in converted attic spaces where seating is at a premium.

The space beneath the window seat is a great storage spot. Here we see open storage used for books. Another option is to construct the window seat on top of a storage box or above a row of built-in, pull-out bins.

Kneewalls on each side of this garage attic room form an alcove,

a gallery of sorts for the resident artist. Kneewalls—short walls that meet the slope of the

roofline in an upstairs room—create interesting angles and shapes.

Skylights

Skylights are tempting in an attic conversion: they're inexpensive and vaguely romantic, but they're not always the best choice. Here are the facts: Dollar for dollar, skylights let in more light than windows, but they lack seasonal efficiency. Conventional, vertical windows let in more sunlight in the winter than do skylights because they catch the low-angled rays of the winter sun. During the summer these same vertical windows cut off the harshest overhead rays of high-angled summer sun. Most skylights, by comparison, let in less light and warmth in the winter, and more in the summer, often funneling in blasts heat along with sunlight. This is not ideal. Tinted glazing and deep, light-diffusing wells can help mitigate this effect, but skylights simply can't duplicate the simple lighting advantages of regular windows.

Skylights do, however, add an architecturally unique top-lighting quality that windows can't touch, and they brighten a room for the least amount of money. For rooms that simply need a source of natural light for aesthetic purposes, skylights are great.

If the roof opening is the same size as the skylight, the light coming through will be focused and direct—basically, creating an intense light shaft on whatever is directly beneath it. For more dispersed light, the ceiling opening needs to be slightly larger than the roof opening. This diffuses the natural light over a larger space.

Installing a skylight in a room that has a finished ceiling with an attic or crawl space above it involves planning both a ceiling opening and a roof opening.

Even better than a skylight in some cases is a "roof window." As the name implies, roof windows follow the slope of the roof, yet they can open and close, providing ventilation, and are installed at eye level so they offer a view.

Tubular skylights use technology that originated with the ancient Egyptians who lined large pipes with highly reflective gold leaf to conduct sunlight into dark stone structures. The modern incarnation uses either rigid or flexible tubing with a highly reflective lining to conduct daylight to a spherical diffuser set into the ceiling of the interior space that needs light.

Stairs

Finished attics require stairs. Pull-down stairs can be used to reach unfinished storage space in a garage attic, but for a finished room, permanent stairs are required. Finding space for the stairs is critical. A standard, straight-run stairway is about 36" wide and 11 to 13' long without landings.

You must allow at least 36" for a landing at the top and bottom.

The handrail must be at a height 30 to 40" above the treads.

Typical building codes require a minimum vertical clearance of 80" at all points on the stairs.

Stair treads must be at least 10" deep.

If you can't spare the space for stairs indoors, an outdoor staircase can be an attractive option. When planning an outdoor staircase, be sure to take both the safety of the staircase and the security of the room into consideration.

Heating/Cooling

An efficient and safe heating and cooling system is a major concern when you convert garage space into living space. You can usually extend your home's existing heating system to the garage if you have one of the following systems: forced-air heat (oil, gas, or electric), electric baseboard heat, or hydronic (hot water) heat. The first step is to have a contractor perform a heat-loss calculation for your home and the garage space you want to heat. This calculation will reveal whether or not your current system can handle the extra load of heating the converted space.

Wall-mounted electric heaters can be installed in a garage no matter what type of heating system is in the rest of the house.

Baseboard heaters come in 4 or 6' lengths, use electricity, are controlled by a thermostat, and come with safety thermal cutoff switches. They can be hard-wired to an electrical circuit or simply plugged into a wall outlet. Though expensive to operate, baseboard heaters are a sensible option for rooms that are not used often, especially on perimeter walls that tend to retain a chill in colder climates.

Direct-vent gas fireplaces don't require chimneys. Combustion air is drawn in from outdoors. It mixes with the gas in the burner, and the flue gases exhaust back outdoors. They use sealed combustion, so the combustion process is totally separate from the room air. Some gas fireplaces include a fan to distribute warmed air and increase heating efficiency. Compared to a traditional fireplace that requires wood, a chimney, and constant maintenance, gas fireplaces are safe, efficient, and draft free.

A ceiling fan can significantly reduce air temperature on a hot day and help distribute heat on a cold day. The fan should be mounted at the highest point on the ceiling.

Electricity

The appropriate wiring scheme for a converted garage depends entirely on how the space will be used and what appliances and devices will be installed there. If the electrical needs of the new space are minimal, an existing circuit may serve. If the demands are more involved, plan on mounting a subpanel in the garage and running one or more circuits from the service entrance panel to the subpanel.

This subpanel operates circuits for the furnace, air conditioner, and other electrical needs in this garage. Installing a subpanel is somewhat advanced electrical work. Hire an electrician for this task unless you're a very experienced do-it-yourselfer.

Part of this garage will be for parking; the other part will be a home spa that features a large jetted tub. Electricity will be routed from the service entrance panel in the house, through underground cables, to the subpanel being installed in the garage.

Running cable from the house to a detached garage is not particularly difficult, but it's important to check local codes. Most codes require UF (underground feed) cable to be buried at least 12" below the ground if you have conduit or other protection, otherwise the trench needs to be at least 24" deep. Consider covering your cable with rot-resistent boards before piling the dirt back on top of it to keep the cable from being inadvertently damaged by a shovel or other implement at some point in the future.

*Design*Wise

Susan Nackers Ludwig
Rehkamp Larson Architects Inc.
Minneapolis, MN

• Check local building codes before you begin any garage conversion project. Codes may require replacement parking spaces or upgraded mechanical systems. There also may be restrictions on how the space can actually be used.

• Try using alternative materials to finish the walls and ceilings. For example, veneered plywood or wood boards can give the space a unique texture and a warm, cozy feeling.

• Give the converted garage space a new feel by staining or painting the concrete floor a fun new color.

• Consider how the new space will be used. Does it need access to the outside? Try replacing the overhead garage door with French doors.

• Instead of building solid walls to divide up space or enclose storage, try large sliding panels or hanging fabric curtains.

• To help integrate the new garage spaces with the house, raise the floor level of the garage to meet the floor level of the existing house. This is a perfect opportunity to install in-floor heating!

• Garages typically have small windows that provide little natural light. Brighten up the spaces by adding skylights, enlarging the existing windows, and replacing the old garage door opening with large windows.

• Consider the site implications of the conversion project. Replace the old driveway access with an area of plantings. If there is still an outside connection to the space, try replacing the driveway with a patio.

Flooring

One flooring option for a converted garage is simply covering the concrete floor with carpeting or rugs. If you live in a temperate climate or have an efficient heating system, this may be sufficient. The room below was originally part of a two-car garage that has been converted to a one-car garage and an attached studio. The floor was sealed with a layer of epoxy and covered with area rugs.

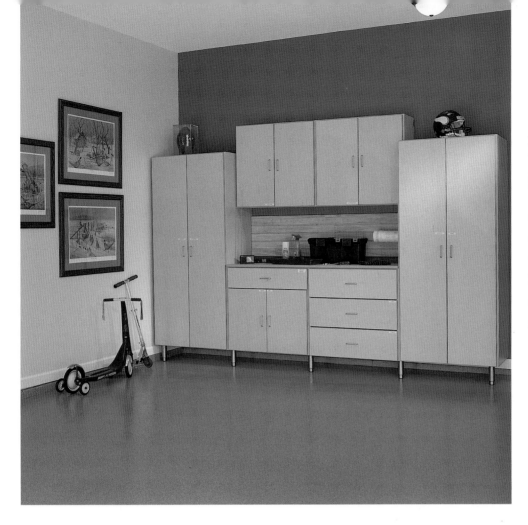

If your converted garage space will be subjected to **skateboards**, scooters, or such juvenile vehicular conveniences, look for a strong two-coat epoxy that offers a durable finish and cleans easily.

IdeaWise

An excellent choice in damp climates or climates with extreme temperature swings is to install a floating subfloor over a concrete floor.

A floating subfloor is more work, costs more to install, and raises the floor height more than a regular subfloor. However, because it's not nailed in place, the floating subfloor can withstand quite a bit of weather- and moisture-related movement without damage to floor coverings installed over it.

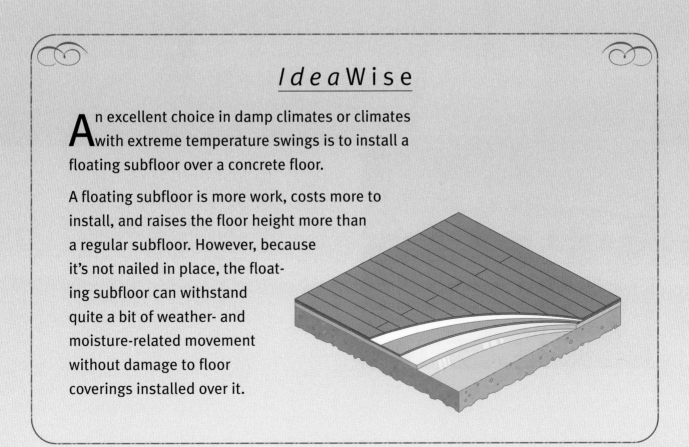

When converting their older era detached garage into a home office, these homeowners decided to install wood flooring over the original concrete garage floor. If you're contemplating a similar flooring adventure, your first step is to make sure the concrete is dry.

The coils you see here will heat the floor of the spa area of this converted garage. Floor heating systems can be installed under tile, natural stone, hardwood, carpet, and floating wood floors. These systems are somewhat expensive to buy and install, so you need to weigh the benefits (it's maintenance free!) against the additional cost. You can choose between electric or hydronic under-floor heating.

Radiant heat keeps bare feet toasty warm after stepping out of the tub in this converted garage.

Insulation

The three most common types of insulation in garage conversions are fiberglass, cellulose, and rigid panels of foam or polystyrene.

If the framing is exposed (either because you've torn down the walls and ceilings or haven't erected them yet) it's relatively easy to add fiberglass batts or rigid panel insulation. Fiberglass is the least expensive; foam insulation, on the other hand, comes in greater R-values per inch of thickness.

If you don't want to rip the walls and ceilings off your garage space, you can insulate with blown-in cellulose. Cellulose can only be blown into sealed cavities. This means cutting small (3") holes in the stud bays then packing insulation into the holes through a hose connected to a rented blower. There are trained insulation contractors to do the job if you lack the patience, confidence, or time to do it yourself.

When you're working with fiberglass insulation, you must wear eye protection, a dust mask, gloves, and make sure your arms and legs are covered completely. Airborne fiberglass fragments irritate skin, eyes, and lungs at the very least, and frequent exposure can present more serious health problems.

Superior insulation results in superior comfort and energy efficiency for the finished space shown at right.

Plumbing

There are two basic phases to any plumbing project: rough plumbing and finishing work. Even for those experienced in maintenance work—leaky pipes, clogged drains, and the like—rough plumbing is tricky. If you have an older home with cast iron pipes, proceed with caution: Cast iron shatters easily without the right tools. On the other hand, even a novice can replace, move, and refit plastic pipes if the waste stack is plastic and the drainpipe is easily accessible. Bottom line: If you're not entirely confident of your plumbing abilities, hire a plumber to tackle the rough work, then do the finish work yourself, if you like.

Proper plumbing enhances converted garage space. Here, kennel space adjoins a shower designed to be convenient for pets and people alike. The bathroom at right was added as part of the spa conversion shown on pages 111 and 113.

CHAPTER 5

Approach

How inviting is your home? This is not a rhetorical question; it's an exercise. Step out beyond your driveway, across the street if necessary, and take in your property from a distance. Imagine you've never seen this place before. Is it welcoming? Does it express your sensibilities? And what does this have to do with garages? Absolutely nothing—unless your garage is visible from the street. Most garages constitute a substantial part of the house's exterior.

Life is a rush. Literally. The never-ending to-do list barks out orders, and we obey. Most of us are exhausted by the time we pull up to our homes at the end of the day. The physical approach to the home shapes our mental and emotional approach to being home.

What happens when you approach your hard-earned portion of this world—your home? If the garage door is an ugly, uninviting, hard, cold expanse of steel, there's no welcome there. If the driveway is crumbling, potholed, dark and foreboding, or dangerous when wet, there's no welcome there. Your transition from the outside world to your private life continues the tension you'd be better off leaving at the doorstep. All this means is that you've got a problem and it's time to fix it.

In this chapter, we'll approach your approach with a fresh eye toward function as well as form.

Garage Doors

The single slab of steel that formerly passed for a garage door is on its way out of the American cityscape. So what's in? A trend in garage design is to keep the style of the garage consistent with that of the house. No longer an unsightly appendage, the garage is being integrated into the larger architectural theme of the residence.

The graceful arch of this garage door blends perfectly with the Spanish-style house and garage.

This log-cabin style garage blends seamlessly into this idyllic setting.

With section panels on a garage door, you run the risk of pinching a finger. Seek out "pinch resistant" design if you're interested in this kind of door.

Here, a simple paint job is all that's needed to create stylistic integrity.

The repetition of architectural details, accent colors, even window dimensions and design confer a certain elegance to these homes. In older homes, the inevitable restoration of a very old garage brings opportunity to finesse the exterior.

From an old cloth blueprint found in their attic, these homeowners learned what the original garage doors on their home looked like when their home was first built. To preserve the historical accuracy of the house, they had a new garage door built to look exactly like the original. The only difference is that the original door slid sideways to open; this door opens by rolling up.

Beautiful homes deserve beautiful garages.

Here, mullioned windows on the garage door echo the windows on the rest of the house.

These ornate garage doors help this modern addition fit in with an older home. The high windows are an added bonus, letting in light without allowing unwanted visitors a peak.

Custom windows contribute to the
illusion that there are two separate doors.
Actually, this is one, double-wide door. The
manufacturer used paint-grade overlay material
to create the façade.

The traditional appearance of this brick two story
is enhanced by an overhead garage door designed to look like three
sets of French doors from the outside.

Nylon rollers are quieter than steel rollers.

Opaque glass lets light into the garage but protects its contents from being identified from outside.

If you have a green thumb or can hire one,
use landscaping elements to create a unified
aesthetic between the garage and home.

*The three garage planters establish a pattern that is
repeated in the perimeter planters under the pergola.
The eye follows the interspersed green of the vines
from garage to walkway to house.*

The shingles are another feature that unify the visual presentation of the garage and the house.

*Design*Wise

Robert Gerloff
Robert Gerloff Residential Architects
Minneapolis, MN

• Finish the exterior of the garage to match the exterior of your house as closely as possible. Use matching siding, matching windows, matching roofing, and matching paint colors. Don't use cheap materials just because it's a garage.

• Use high-quality wood garage doors on a more traditional house or high-quality aluminum doors on a more modern house. Think of the garage door as the equivalent of the front door of the house. Use as much glass as possible on the garage doors to let as much natural light into the garage as possible. Sandblast or "frost" the glass to keep people from seeing inside the garage.

• Add windows, garden doors, flower boxes, trellises, and other architectural details from your house to break up the long blank walls and tie the garage to the house.

• Think of the area in front of the garage doors not as driveway, but as a multi-purpose outdoor court-yard space. Change paving materials from a driveway material to a concrete paver or brick ma-terial, something that says this space can be used for more than parking the car.

• Think of your garage as a small version of your house, a Mama Bear to your house's Papa Bear. Thinking this way will help you match details and colors from the garage to the house

• Use several narrow single garage doors rather than one wider double garage door to help break down the scale of the garage.

Driveways

According to the National Association of Home Builders (NAHB), about 60 percent of driveways are poured concrete; another 20 percent are asphalt, about 10 percent are gravel, and the remaining 10 percent are made from brick, patterned concrete, or pre-cast pavers. Cost, climate, and local custom all play a part in the choice of driveway materials.

If you plan for a turn-around area, you won't have to back into the street. For most residential driveways, you only need a 15-ft. radius at the turning point.

Starting at about 50¢ per square foot, gravel is the least expensive option for a driveway. The problem with gravel is that it's a relatively high-maintenance surface, and it's difficult to keep gravel on grades steeper than about 8 percent. Another problem is that gravel is difficult to contain and can wreck your lawn mower if it migrates into the lawn.

Asphalt starts at about $1 per square foot, which makes it relatively inexpensive. It isn't as durable as concrete and can soften and get gouged rather easily in hot temperatures. It's a more practical choice in cold climates. The dark color absorbs heat from the sun, helping to melt snow and ice.

Concrete costs twice as much as asphalt at roughly $2 per square foot. Unlike asphalt, you can theoretically—given a bit of talent and a few willing friends—pour the concrete yourself. Without labor costs, the price is roughly the same as asphalt—about $1 per square ft.

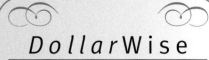

*Dollar*Wise

Sure, cracked concrete is unattractive, but replacing a driveway can be an expensive proposition. Before you decide to replace that slab, take a second look. If the surface is damaged but the concrete is still structurally sound, save money by resurfacing rather than replacing it.

Purchase sand-mix concrete or a masonry product designed specifically for resurfacing. The new layer will bond better if it's packed down, so use a dry, stiff mixture that can be compacted with a shovel.

Modern concrete has many faces.

Starting at about $5.50 per square foot, exposed aggregate concrete
has a more textured look and feel than poured concrete and offers better traction. As the name
would suggest, rounded, decorative aggregate is mixed in with the concrete. When the concrete is partially set, the topmost layer is scrubbed off to expose the aggregate.

Patterned (or stamped) concrete is standard cement concrete that's been colored and or stained and imprinted with a pattern prior to curing. This is not a job for do-it-yourselfers. Contractors use heavy rollers to imprint the patterns onto the wet cement. The stamping process requires specialized skill and training. Patterned concrete starts at about $6 per square foot.

IdeaWise

When building a driveway, add an extra layer of Dense-Graded Aggregate (DGA) at the bottom of the driveway where the driveway meets the street. The extra layer only needs to extend about a car length up the driveway. This area receives the heaviest use. A couple extra tons of DGA may prevent damage to the surface layer of your driveway in the future.

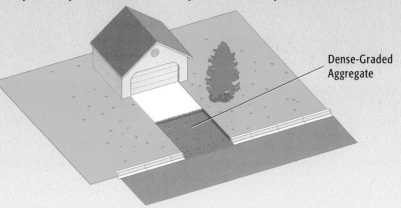

Dense-Graded Aggregate

Cobblestone pavers date back to the ancient Romans. Nowadays, most pavers take the form of bricks or pre-cast concrete pavers. Bricks and pavers are small and fairly easy to install, but time consuming. In addition to the pavers or bricks, you'll need a carefully prepared base. Bricks are about $1.50 per square foot. Concrete pavers average about $3.50 per square foot. If you hire out the labor, count on paying about $6 per square foot.

Combining materials, such as the bricks and exposed aggregate here, creates striking driveways.

Pavers are commonly used in temperate climates where they're not often exposed to freeze/thaw cycles. They can, however, be used in cold climates as long as the base is properly prepared.

Truly inspired homeowners may want to integrate greenery between pavers to emphasize the pattern in their driveway design. An awesome effect!

Low, creeping plants are slowly filling the spaces between the slabs in the less-trafficked part of this integrated driveway and sidewalk.

Spaces between pavers must be filled with durable plants that will thrive despite driveway traffic.

Lighting

Well-planned exterior lighting can make the approach to your home
safer in the dark and more inviting.

*Stair lighting is especially important to consider
when you're setting up lighting for safety.*

*Post sconces and wall lanterns above eye level to
wash walls with light without uncomfortable glare.*

Use lighting to accent the architectural details that make your home unique. Keep lights focused downward to avoid glare.

Avoid extremes of light and shadow. Steady light is much more effective than spotlight-type beams of bright light.

Warm, inviting light creates a safe, welcoming exterior.

Resource Guide

A listing of resources for information, designs, and products found in _IdeaWise Garages_.

Introduction

page 7: Garage storage by:
California Closets
Locations throughout the United States and Canada. For a complimentary in-home design consultation call
800-274-6754 or visit
www.calclosets.com

The Multi-Use Garage

page 15: Garage Cabinet Design by:
Doug Kadan/KADANGROUP
832 Purser Dr.suite 203
Raleigh, NC 27603
919-779-4239
contact sales@kadangroup.com
www.kadangroup.com
www.kadangarage.com

page 16-17: Garage by:
Gladiator Garageworks/
Whirlpool Corporation
1-866-342-4089
www.gladiatorgw.com

page 18: Garage design by:
GarageTek
5 Aerial way, Suite 200
Syasset, NY 11791
866-664-2724
www.garagetek.com

page 20: Garage design by:
St. Croix Beautiful Garages
1712 Stag Circle
Hudson, WI 54016
715-386-2470

page 21 (top): Garage floor by
Better Life Technology, LLC
9820 Pflumm Road
Lenexa, Kansas 66215
913-894-0403 ext. 21
www.bltllc.com

page 21 (bottom): Garage design by:
GarageTek
5 Aerial way, Suite 200
Syasset, NY 11791
866-664-2724
www.garagetek.com

page 23: Garage storage by:
California Closets
Locations throughout the United States and Canada. For a complimentary in-home design consultation call
800-274-6754 or visit
www.calclosets.com

page 24 (top): Hoist by
The Complete Garage
Crossroads Center
1593 Highway 7
Hopkins, MN 55305
952-935-5200
www.thecompletegarage.com

page 24: (bottom) Hoist by:
GarageTek
5 Aerial way, Suite 200
Syasset, NY 11791
866-664-2724
www.garagetek.com

page 25: Garage storage lift system by:
Loft-it/Tivan, Inc.
5305 Frost Point
Prior Lake, MN 55372-1906
952-440-8233
www.loft-it.com

pages 26-27 (both): Design by:
Richard Laffin Architects,
Trehus Builders
275 East 4th St., Northwestern Bldg. #740
St. Paul, MN 55101
651-312-0988
  3017 4th Ave. S.
  Minneapolis, MN 55408
  612-729-2992
  www.trehusbuilders.com

pages 28-29 (all): Design by:
Locus Architecture
1500 Jackson St. N.E., Ste. 333
Minneapolis, MN 55413
612-706-5600
www.locusarchitecture.com

page 31: Garage storage by:
California Closets
Locations throughout the United States and Canada. For a complimentary in-home design consultation call
800-274-6754 or visit
www.calclosets.com

page 32 (both): Garage design by:
GarageTek
5 Aerial way, Suite 200
Syasset, NY 11791
866-664-2724
www.garagetek.com

page 33 (both): Storage, organization, display by:
storeWALL™
1699 N. Astor
Milwaukee, WI 53202
414-224-0878
www.storewall.com

pages 34-35 (all):
Garage cabinet design by:
Don Mitchell/Mitchell Garage Cabinet Systems
800-350-MGCS
www.MitchellGarageCabinetSystems.com

pages 36-37: (all) Design by:
Schrock and
DeVetter Architects
3101 E. Franklin Ave.
Minneapolis, MN 55406
612-338-8225
www.sdva.com

Garage Workshops

page48-49 (both): Garage cabinet design by:
Don Mitchell/
Mitchell Garage Cabinet Systems
800-350-MGCS
www.MitchellGarageCabinetSystems.com

page 50-51 (both): Garage cabinet design by:
Don Mitchell/
Mitchell Garage Cabinet Systems
800-350-MGCS
www.MitchellGarageCabinetSystems.com

pages 52-53: Garage by:
Gladiator Garageworks/
Whirlpool Corporation
866-342-4089
www.gladiatorgw.com

page 55: Garage storage by:
Mill's Pride
2 Easton Oval, Suite 310
Columbus OH 43219
800-441-0337
Mill's Pride cabinets available
exclusively at Home Depot
www.millspride.com

page 58-59 (all): Storage, organization, display by:
storeWALL™
1699 N. Astor
Milwaukee, WI 53202
414-224-0878
www.storewall.com

page 60: Woodworking studio designed by:
Dave Vincent
Binkys Woodworking
www.binkyswoodworking.com

pages 61-62 (all): Garage cabinet design by:
Don Mitchell/Mitchell Garage Cabinet Systems
800-350-MGCS
www.MitchellGarageCabinetSystems.com

page 64 (top): Woodworking studio designed by:
Dave Vincent
Binkys Woodworking
www.binkyswoodworking.com

page 64 (bottom): Garage cabinet design by:
Don Mitchell/Mitchell Garage Cabinet Systems
800-350-MGCS
www.MitchellGarageCabinetSystems.com

Resource Guide
(continued)

page 100: Design by:
Awad Koontz Architects Builders, Inc.
6603 Queen Ave. S., Ste. 5R
Minneapolis, MN 55423
612-243-0540
www.awadandkoontz.com

page 101: Design by:
Robert Gerloff Residential Architects
4007 Sheridan Avenue South
Minneapolis, MN 55410
612-927-5913

page 102: (top) Design by:
Randy Walker, Walker Design Studio
3616 26th Ave. S.
Minneapolis, MN 55406
612-282-9820

page 102 (bottom): Design by:
Rosemary McMoniga, AIA/McMonigal
Architects, LLC
1224 Marshall St. N.E. #400
Minneapolis, MN 55413

page 104-105 (both): Design by Richard
Laffin Architects, Trehus Builders
275 East 4th St., Northwestern Bldg. #740
St. Paul, MN 55101
651-312-0988

page 106: Design by:
Jack Barkla
4252 Drew Ave S.
Minneapolis, MN 55410
612-338-2092

page 107: Garage by:
St. Croix Beautiful Garages
1712 Stag Circle
Hudson, WI 54016
715-386-2470

page 108 (both): Design by:
Randy Walker, Walker Design Studio
3616 26th Ave. S.
Minneapolis, MN 55406
612-282-9820

Conversion to Living Space

page 84: Design by:
Robert Gerloff Residential Architects
4007 Sheridan Avenue South
Minneapolis, MN 55410
612-927-5913

pages 88-89 (all): Design by:
Robert Gerloff Residential Architects
4007 Sheridan Avenue South
Minneapolis, MN 55410
612-927-5913

pages 90-91 (both): Design by:
Awad Koontz Architects Builders, Inc.
6603 Queen Ave. S., Ste. 5R
Minneapolis, MN 55423
612-243-0540
www.awadandkoontz.com

page 92: Garage doors by:
Designer Doors, Inc.
800-241-0525
www.designerdoors.com

pages 94-95 (both): Garage doors by:
Designer Doors, Inc.
800-241-0525
www.designerdoors.com

pages 96-97 (both): Design by:
Robert Gerloff Residential Architects
4007 Sheridan Avenue South
Minneapolis, MN 55410
612-927-5913

page 98: Design by:
Randy Walker, Walker Design Studio
3616 26th Ave. S.
Minneapolis, MN 55406
612-282-9820

page 99 (all): Windows and suntunnel
skylights by:
VELUX-America, Inc.
450 Old Brickyard Road
Greenwood, SC 29649
800-888-3589
www.VELUXusa.com

page 109 (both): Design by:
Richard Laffin Architects, Trehus
Builders
275 East 4th St., Northwestern Bldg.
#740
St. Paul, MN 55101
651-312-0988
   3017 4th Ave. S.
   Minneapolis, MN 55408
   612-729-2992
   www.trehusbuilders.com

pages 110-111 (both): Design by
Richard Laffin Architects, Trehus
Builders
275 East 4th St., Northwestern Bldg.
#740
St. Paul, MN 55101
651-312-0988
   3017 4th Ave. S.
   Minneapolis, MN 55408
   612-729-2992
   www.trehusbuilders.com

page 112: Design by:
Rehkamp Larson Architects, Inc.
2732 West 43rd St.
Minneapolis, MN 55410
612-285-7275
www.rehkamplarson.com

page 113: Design by: Richard Laffin
Architects, Trehus Builders
275 East 4th St., Northwestern Bldg.
#740
St. Paul, MN 55101
651-312-0988
   3017 4th Ave. S.
   Minneapolis, MN 55408
   612-729-2992
   www.trehusbuilders.com

Approach

page 116: Garage doors by:
Designer Doors, Inc.
800-241-0525
www.designerdoors.com

page 118-119 (both) : Garage doors by:
Designer Doors, Inc.
800-241-0525
www.designerdoors.com

page 120-121 (all): Garage doors by:
Designer Doors, Inc.
800-241-0525
www.designerdoors.com

page 122-123 (both): Garage doors by:
FrenchPorte™ Garage Doors
121 Congressional Lane, Penthouse
Suite
Rockville, MD 20852
866-545-4561
www.frenchporte.com

page 124-125 (both): Design by:
Altus Architecture
www.altusarch.com

page 127 (top): Garage doors by:
Designer Doors, Inc.
800-241-0525
www.designerdoors.com

page 129: Stamped Concrete
Driveway by:
Increte Systems, Inc.
800-752-4626
www.increte.com

Photo Credits

Front cover photo and title page: ©Andrea Rugg.

Back cover photos: (top left) photo courtesy of StoreWALL™; (center) photo courtesy of Designer Doors, Inc.; (top right) Loft-it/Tivan Inc., Prior Lake, MN.; (bottom left); ©2005 California Closet Company, Inc. all rights reserved.

pp.2-3: (top) ©Mitchell Garage Cabinet Systems; (bottom left) ©Andrea Rugg; (bottom right) photo courtesy of Designer Doors, Inc.

pp. 4-5: ©Andrea Rugg.

p. 7: (top) ©Stephen Simpson/Getty Images; (bottom) ©2005 California Closet Company, Inc. all rights reserved.

pp. 8-9: (all) ©Len Jenshel/Diane Cook.

p. 10: ©Yellow Dog Productions/Getty Images.

p. 11: ©Andrea Rugg.

p. 13: ©Andrea Rugg.

p. 15: Photo by DIK Souan Photography/courtesy of Kaden Group.

p. 16-17: Photo courtesy of Gladiator Garageworks by Whirlpool Corporation.

p. 18: Photo courtesy of GarageTek.

p. 19: ©Andrea Rugg.

p. 20: ©Andrea Rugg for Saint Croix Beautiful Garages.

p. 21: (top) Photo courtesy of Better Life Technology, LLC; (bottom) Photo courtesy of GarageTek.

p. 22: ©2005 California Closet Company, Inc. all rights reserved.

p. 24: (top) Photo courtesy of The Complete Garage; (bottom) Photo courtesy of GarageTek.

p. 25: Photo courtesy of Loft-it/Tivan Inc., Prior Lake, MN.

p. 26-27: (both) ©Andrea Rugg for Richard Laffin Architects, Trehus Builders.

p. 28-29: (all) ©Andrea Rugg for Locus Architecture.

p. 30: ©Andrea Rugg.

p. 31: ©2005 California Closet Company, Inc. all rights reserved.

pp. 32-33: Photo courtesy of StoreWALL™.

pp.34-35: (all) Photo courtesy of Mitchell Garage Cabinet Systems.

pp. 36-37: ©Andrea Rugg for Schrock and DeVetter Architects.

pp. 38-39: ©Andrea Rugg.

pp. 40-41: ©Andrea Rugg.

p. 42: ©Lester Lefkowitz/Getty Images.

pp. 44-47: (all) ©Andrea Rugg for artist Steven Swanson.

pp. 48-49: (all) Mitchell Garage Cabinet Systems.

pp. 50-51: Mitchell Garage Cabinet Systems.

pp. 52-53: Photo courtesy of Gladiator Garageworks by Whirlpool Corporation.

p. 54: ©Sergio Piumatti.

p. 55: Photo courtesy of Mill's Pride.

pp. 56-57: ©Sergio Piumatti.

pp. 58-59: (all) Photo courtesy of StoreWALL™.

p. 60: Photo courtesy of Binkys Woodworking/binkys-woodworking.com.

p. 61: (top) Photo courtesy of Mitchell Garage Cabinet Systems.

p. 62: Photo courtesy of Mitchell Garage Cabinet Systems.

p. 63: ©Andrea Rugg.

p. 64: (top) Photo courtesy of Binkys Woodworking/binkyswoodworking.com; (bottom) Photo courtesy of Mitchell Garage Cabinet Systems.

p. 66: ©Brian Vanden Brink.

Index

Also from

CREATIVE PUBLISHING INTERNATIONAL

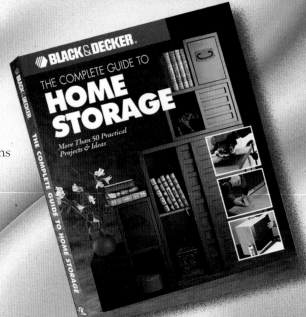

CREATIVE PUBLISHING INTERNATIONAL

18705 LAKE DRIVE EAST
CHANHASSEN, MN 55317

WWW.CREATIVEPUB.COM